Ten, Not Six!

By Carmel Reilly

I see six of us.

Mum, Dad, Liv ...

... Zac and me ...

Zac

me

And here is Pop.

Pop is Mum's dad.

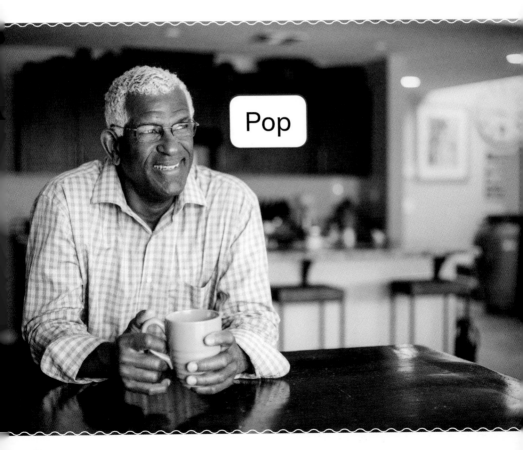

Pop

Pop has a cat, Zan.

Zan sits on Pop's bed.

Zan

Dex and Biz
are Mum's dogs.

Dex runs in the sun.

Biz yaps a lot!

Dex

Yap! Yap!

Biz

Yin is Zac's cat.

She naps in a box.

Yin naps a lot!

Yin

So, is it six of us?

Mum

Dad

Liv

Zac

Pop

me

No!

It is ten, not six!

Zan

Dex

Biz

Yin

CHECKING FOR MEANING

1. Where does Pop's cat sit? *(Literal)*

2. How many dogs does Mum have? What are their names? *(Literal)*

3. Why does the girl think there are ten in the family, not six? *(Inferential)*

EXTENDING VOCABULARY

yum, Yum	How does something taste if we describe it as *yum*? What are other words that we could use instead?
Zac	What sounds are in this name? Find other names in the book that have *x*, *y* or *z* in them.
Yap	What is the meaning of *yap* in this book? What other words can you think of that describe the sound a dog makes?

MOVING BEYOND THE TEXT

1. Why do we sometimes include pets as part of our family?

2. What are other words that describe noises made by animals? E.g. cat – meow; horse – neigh; cow – moo.

3. Where do cats like to sleep and why?

4. Who is in your family? Why?

SPEED SOUNDS

Xx	Yy	Zz		
Kk	Ll	Vv	Qq	Ww
Dd	Jj	Oo	Gg	Uu
Cc	Bb	Rr	Ee	Ff	Hh	Nn
Mm	Ss	Aa	Pp	Ii	Tt

PRACTICE WORDS

Six

yum

Yum

Dex

Zac

Zan

Biz

yaps

Yap

Yin

box